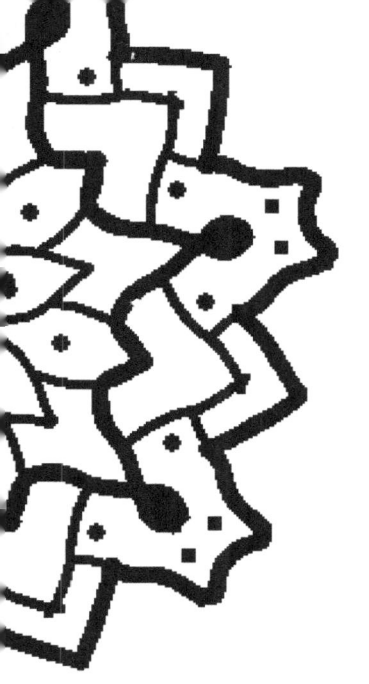

This coloring book belongs to

_____

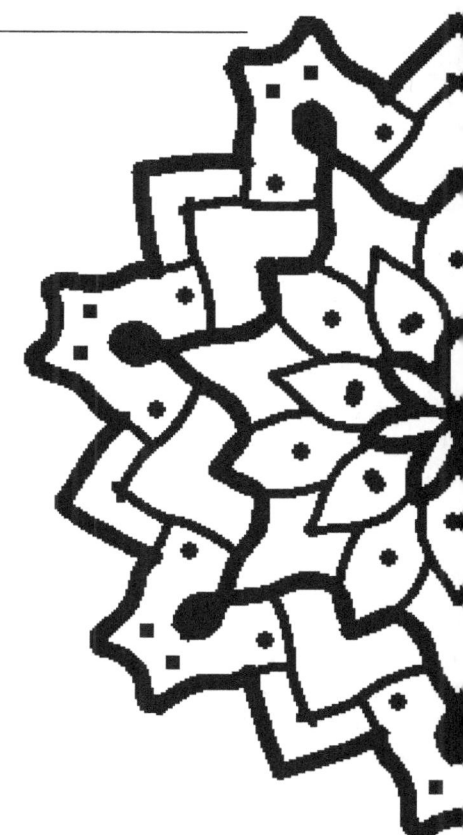

Mandala Illustrations by: Jordon Floyd

2019. All rights reserved. This book may not be reproduced or quoted in whole or part by any means whatsoever.

2019. KINDLE DIRECT PUBLISHING.

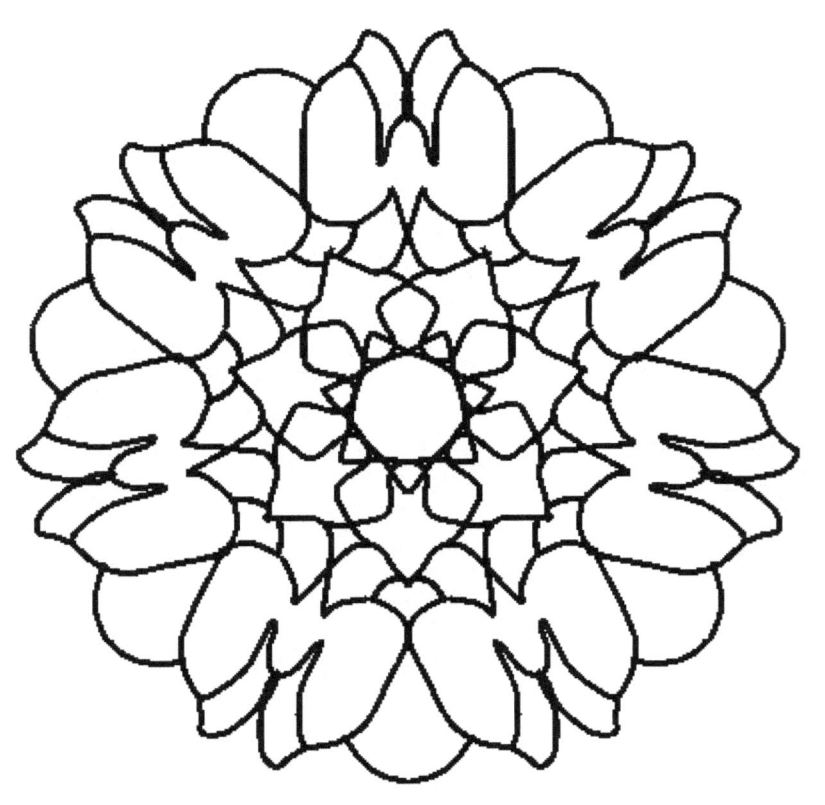

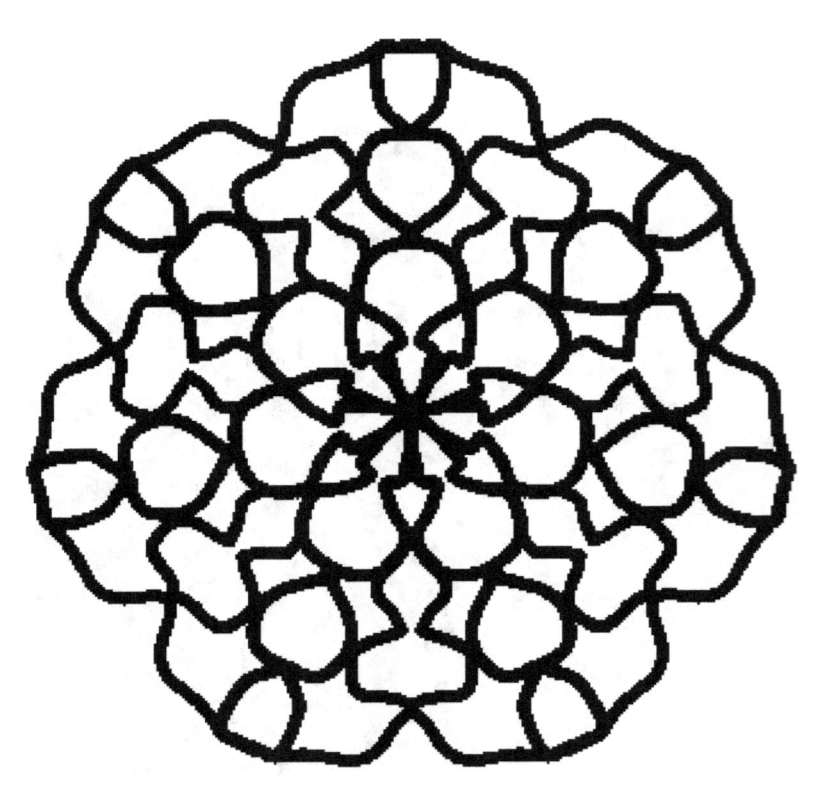

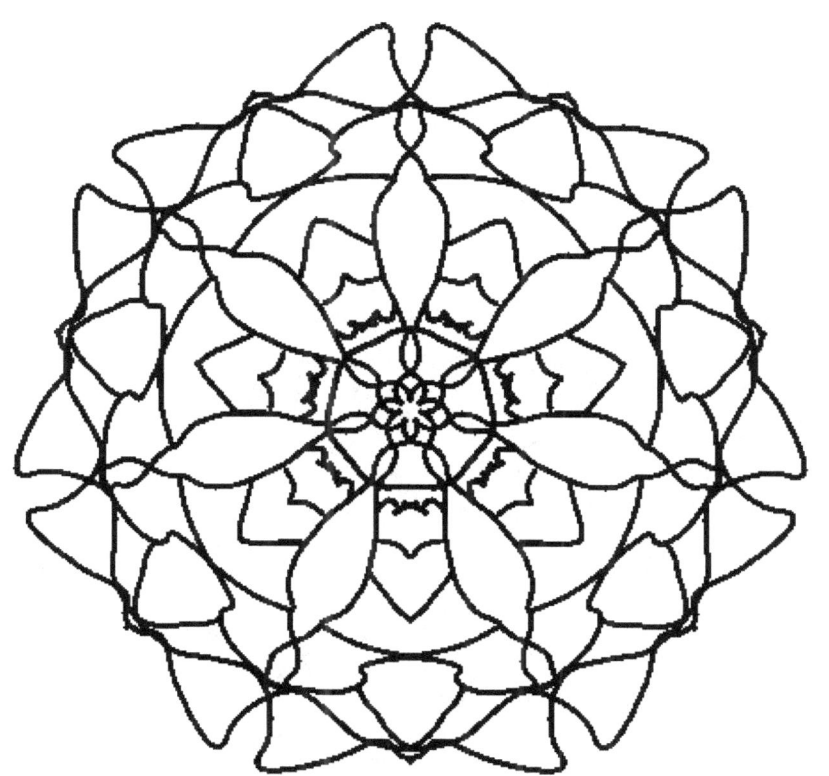

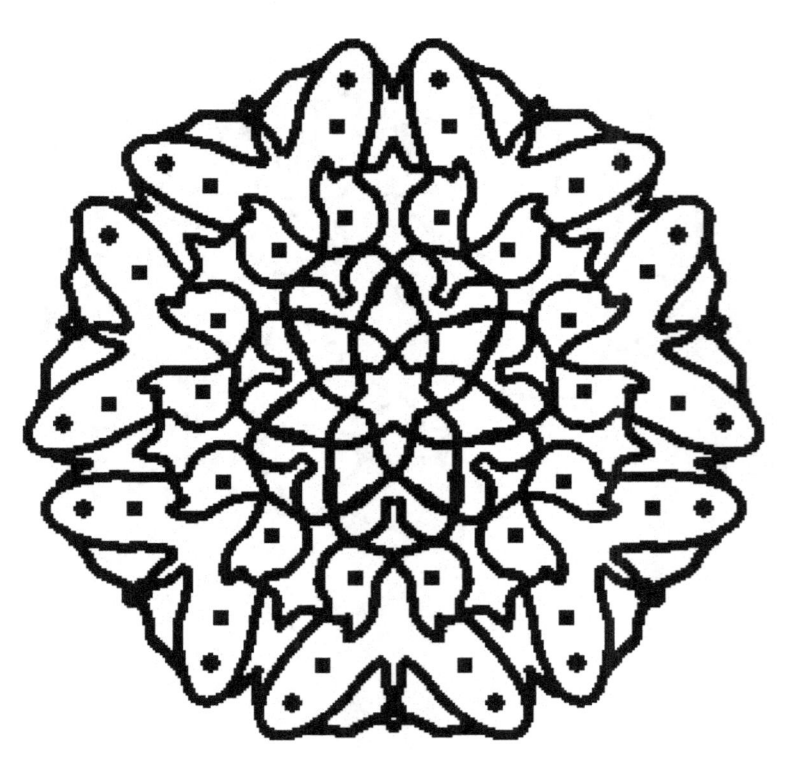

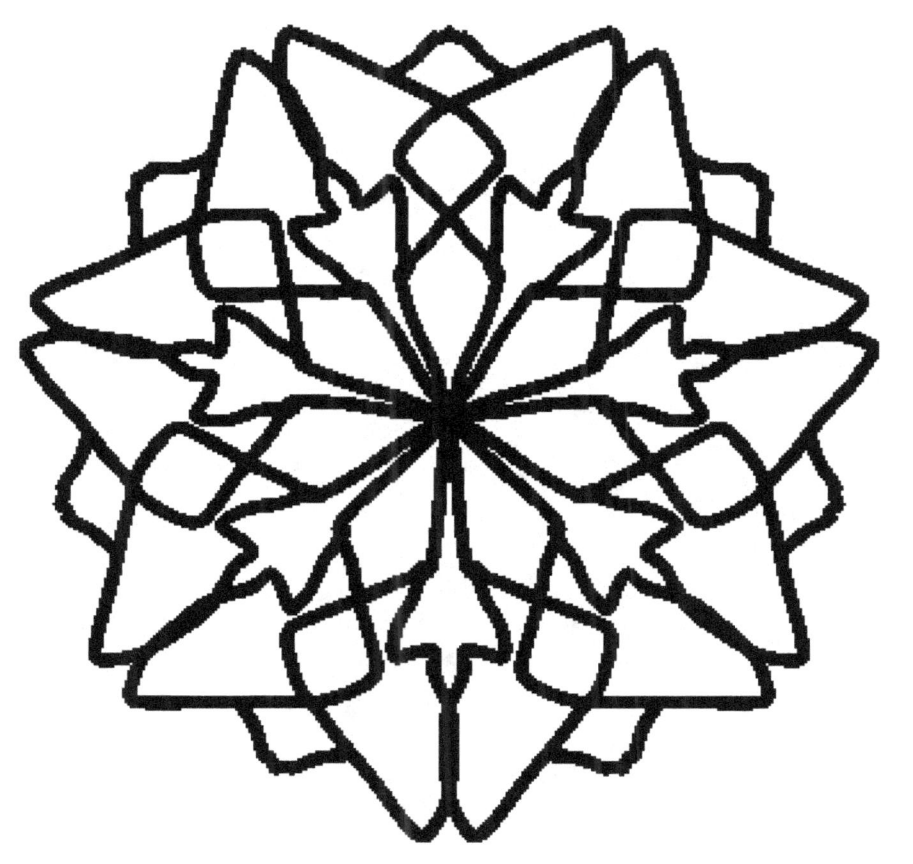

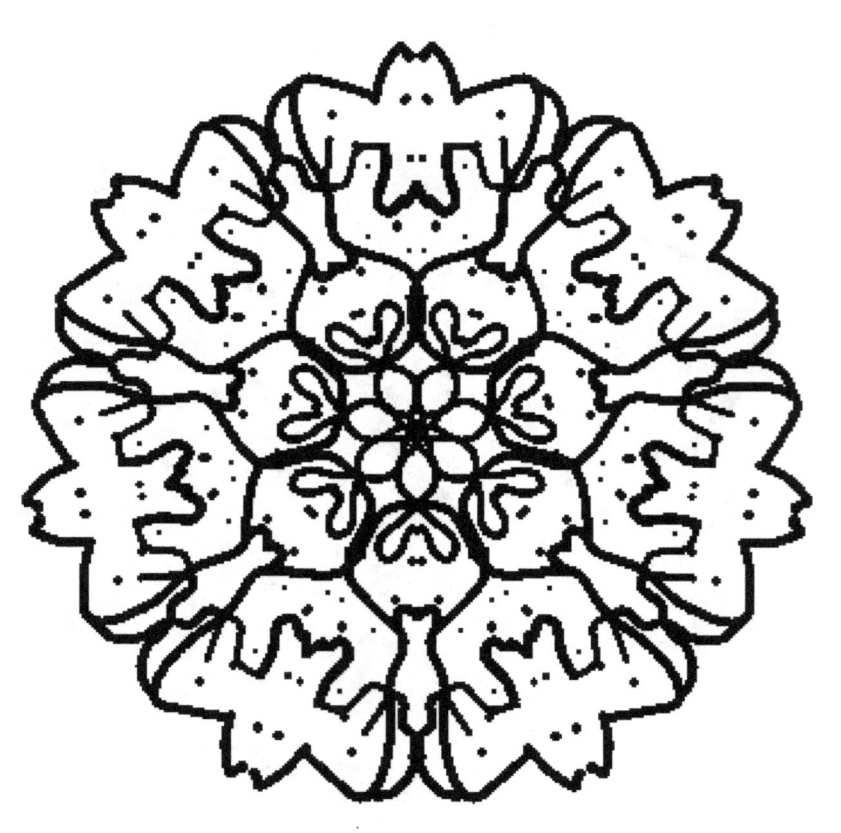

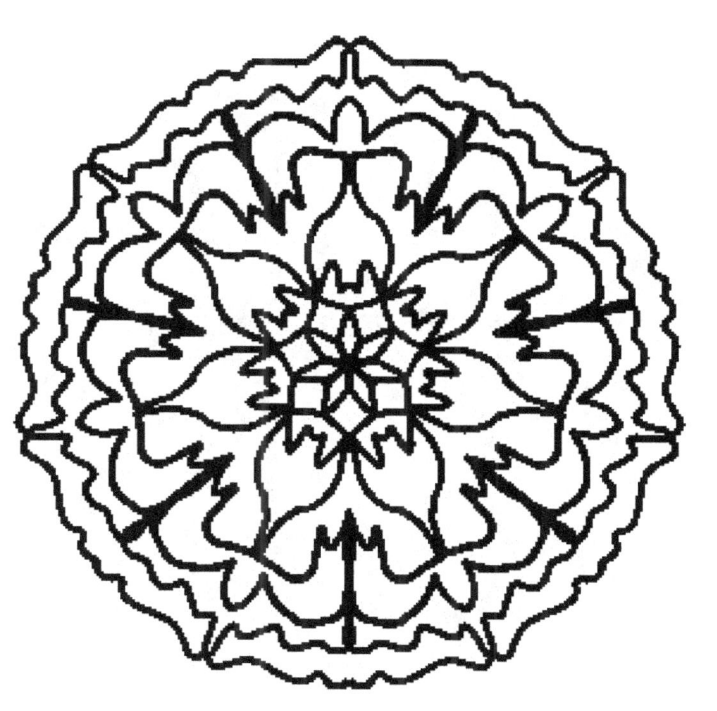

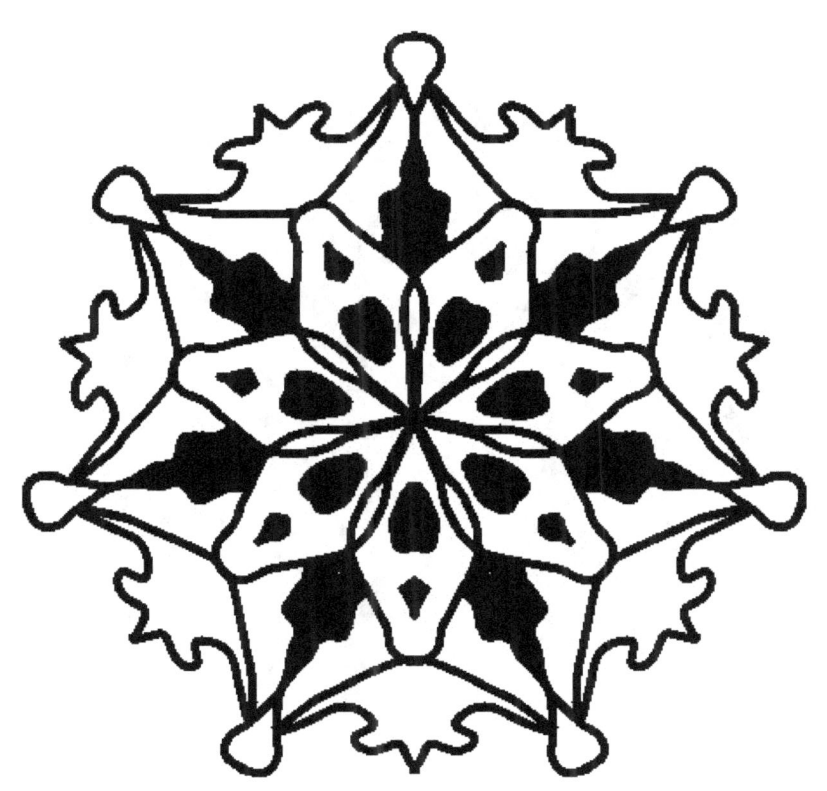

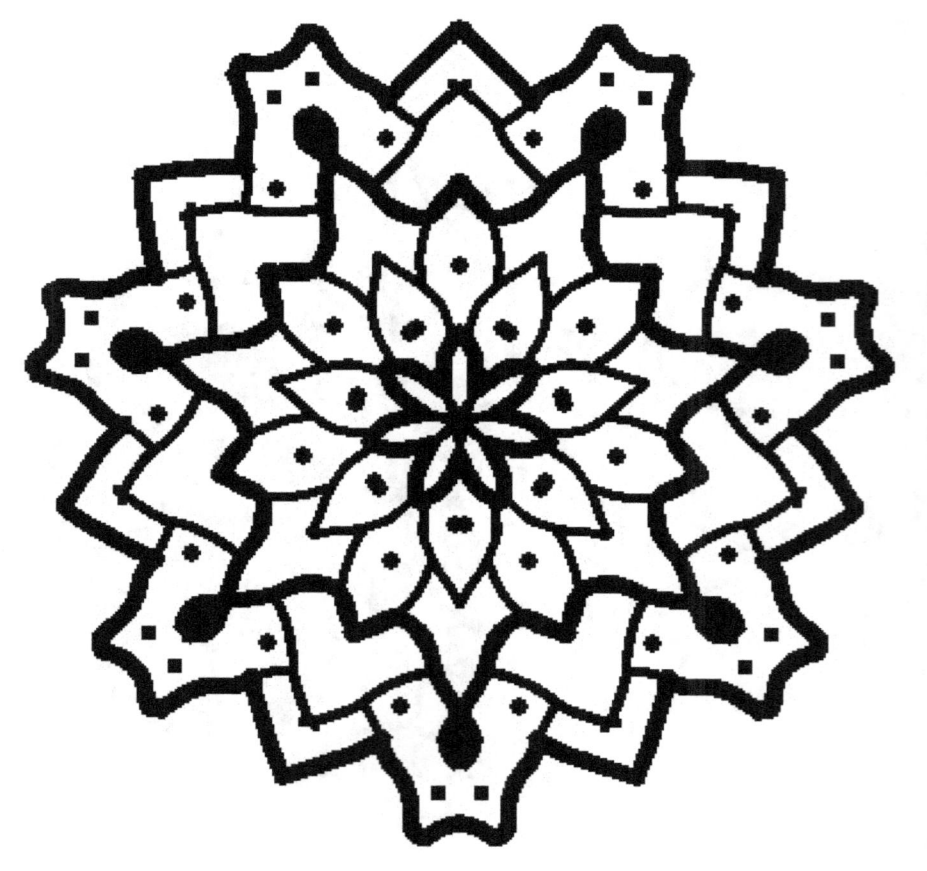

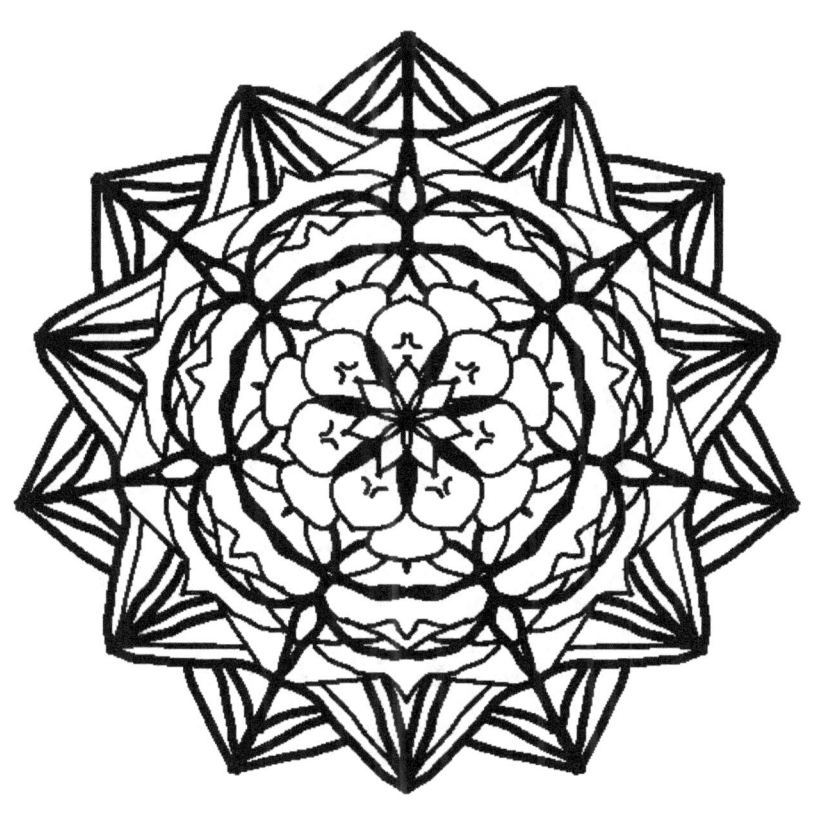

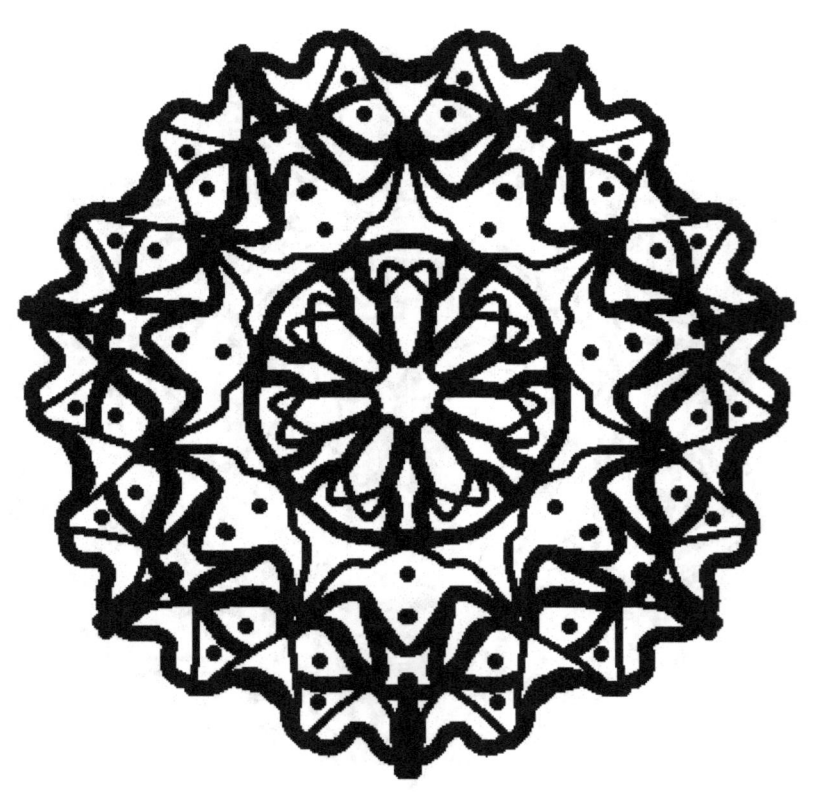

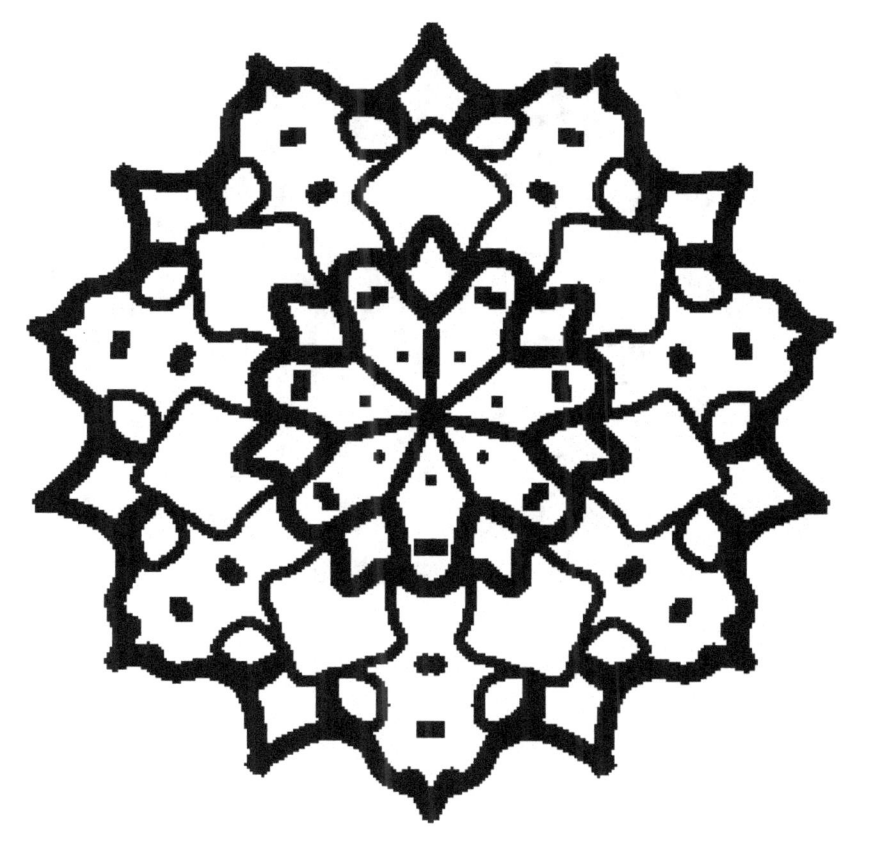

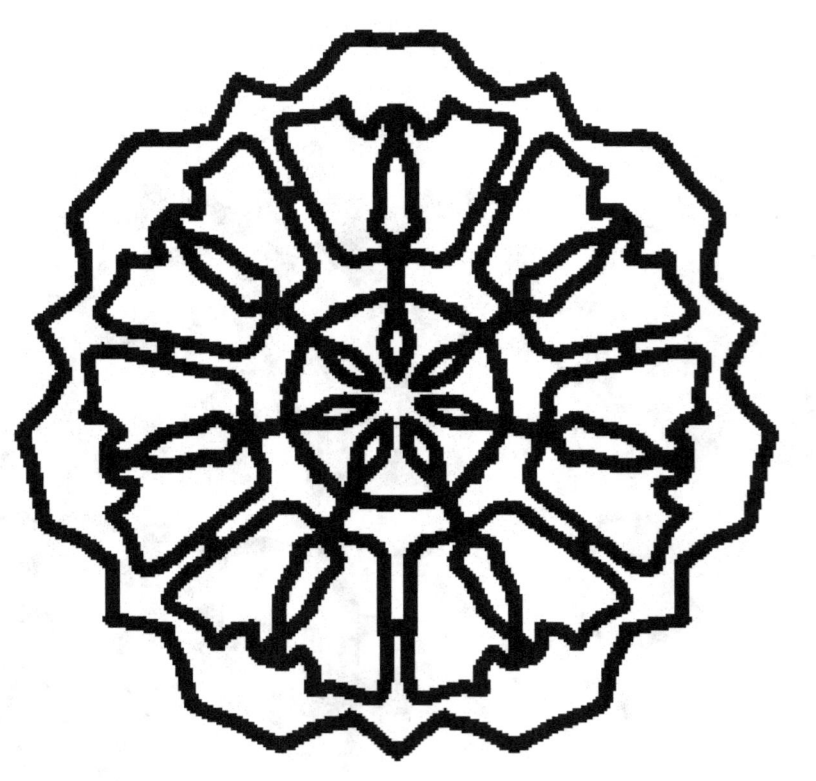

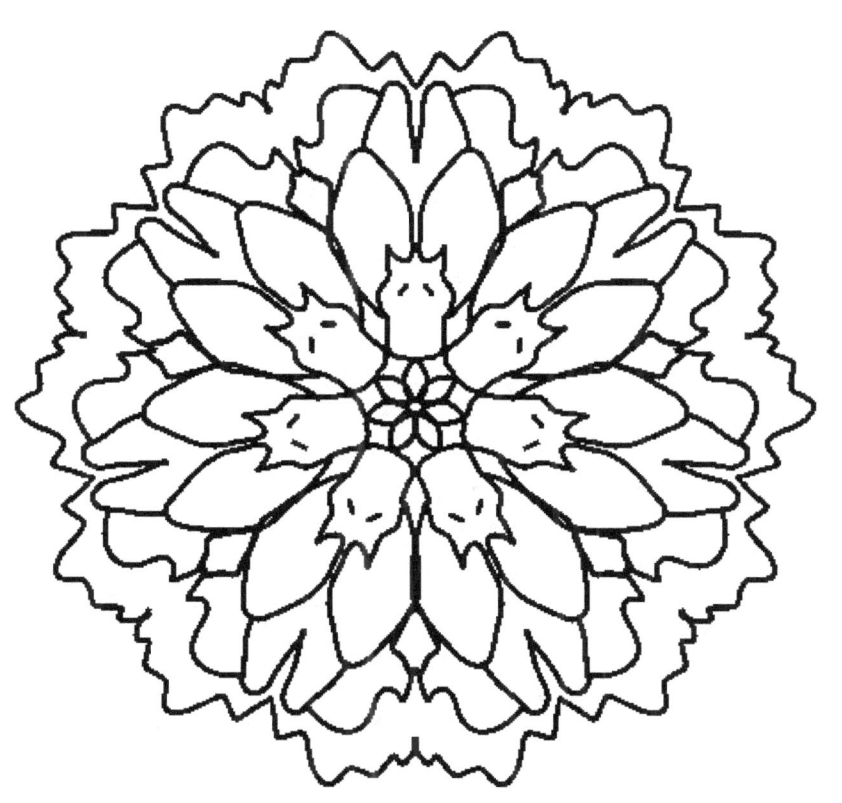

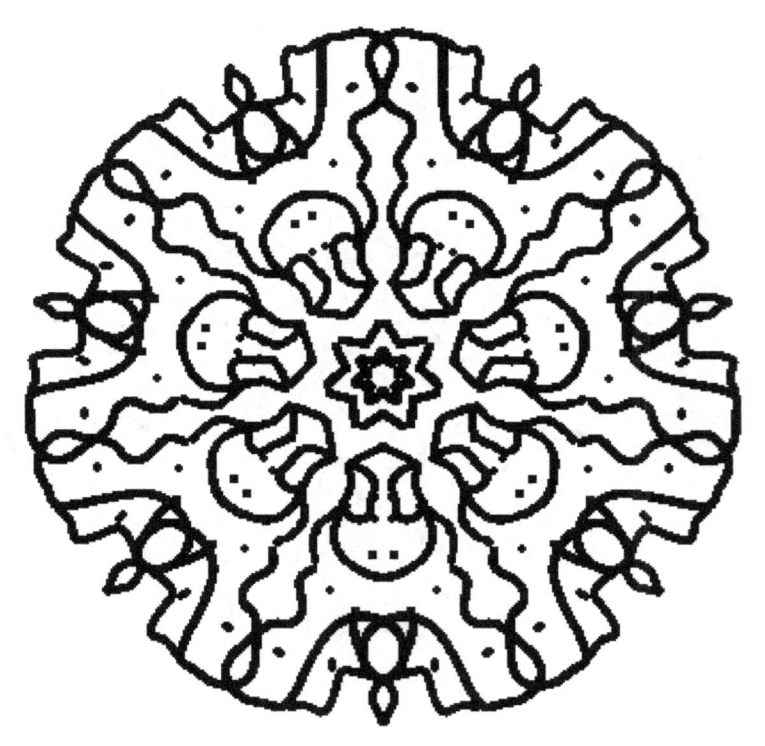

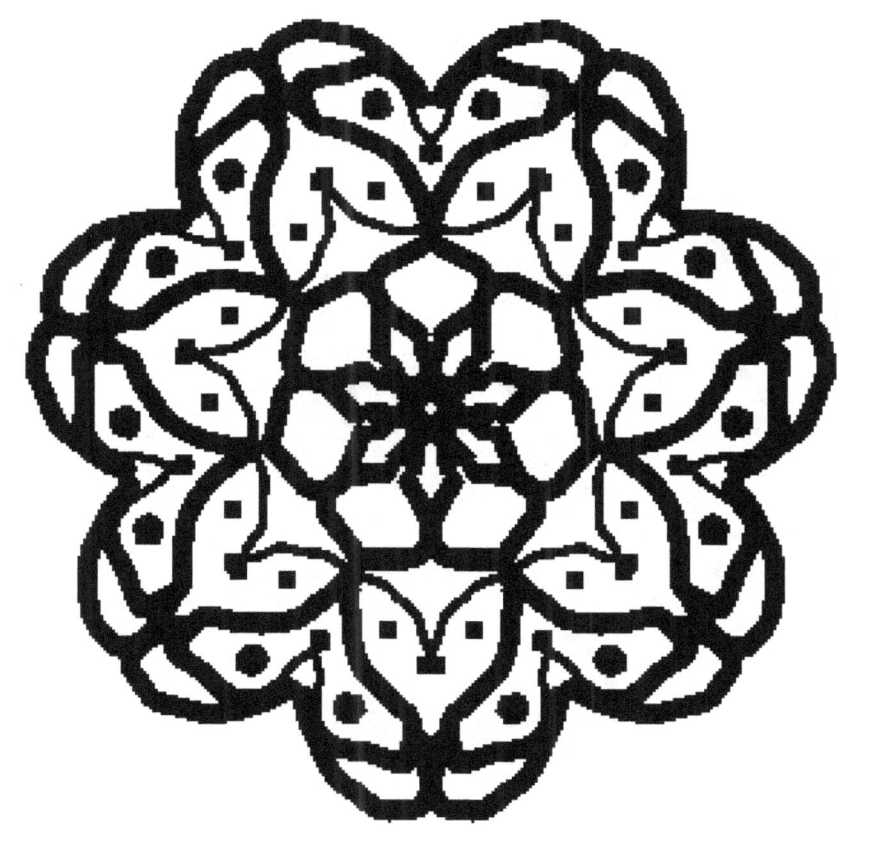

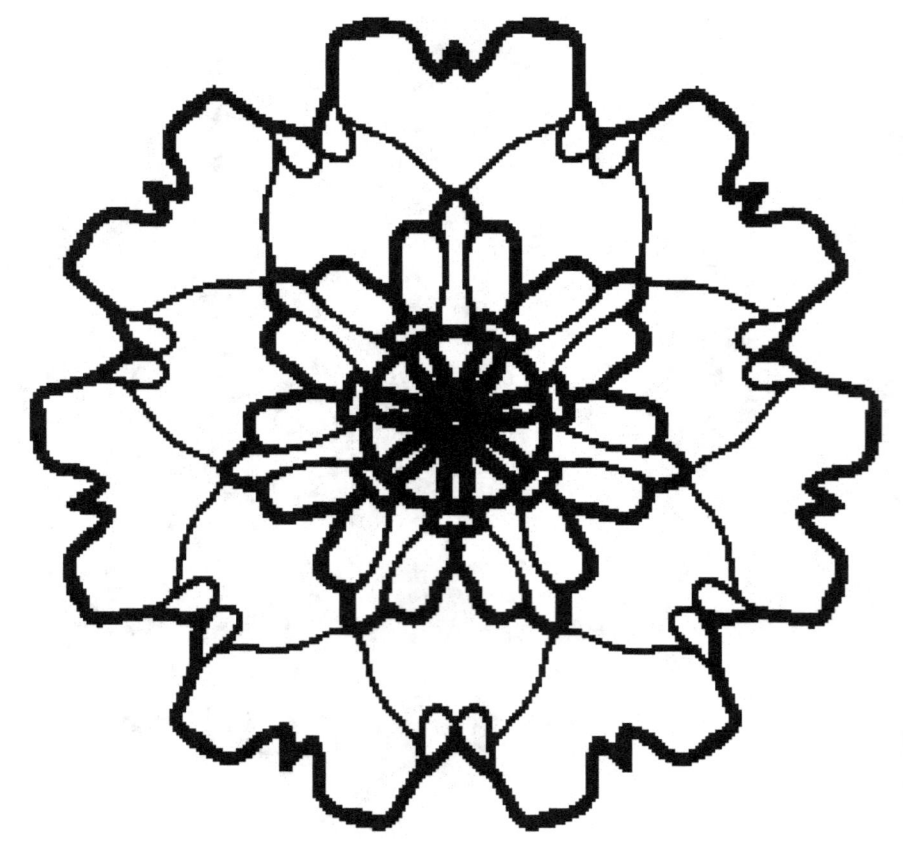

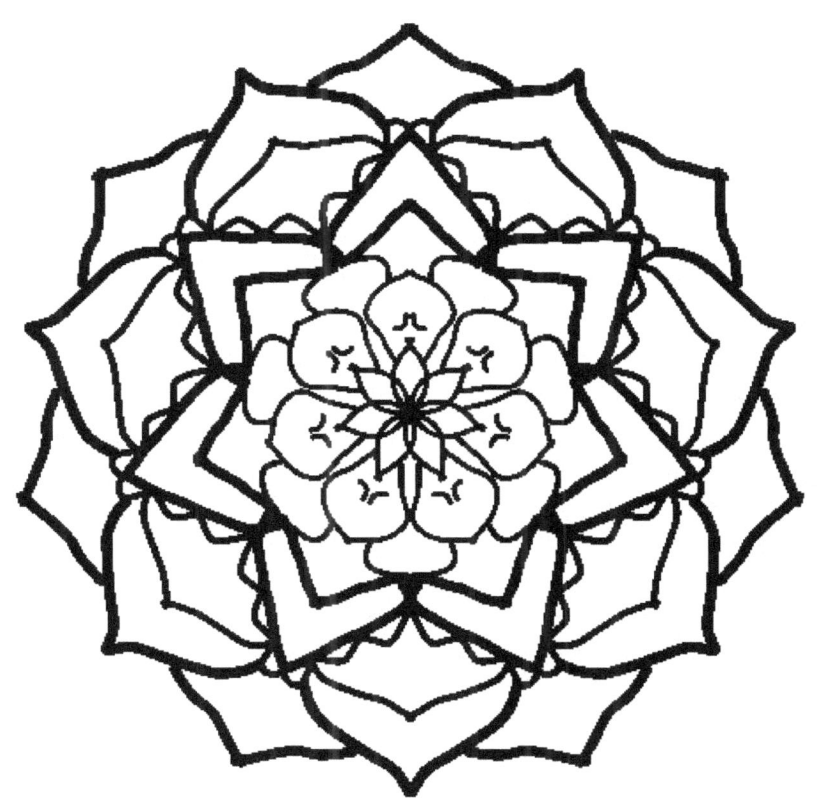

www.ingramcontent.com/pod-product-compliance
Lightning Source LLC
Chambersburg PA
CBHW070802220526
45466CB00013B/2239